G000134533

Sign of the Times

A comedy

Tim Firth

Samuel French — London
www.samuelfrench-london.co.uk

SIGN OF THE TIMES

First presented as *Absolutely Frank* at the Theatre Royal, Windsor on 30th March 2009 with the following cast:

Frank   Stephen Tompkinson
Alan   Tom Shaw

Directed by Peter Wilson
Designed by Morgan Large
Lighting by Tony Simpson
Sound by Theo Holloway

Subsequently presented at the Duchess Theatre, London on 11th March 2011 with the following cast:

Frank   Matthew Kelly
Alan   Gerard Kearns

Directed by Peter Wilson
Designed by Morgan Large
Lighting by Tony Simpson
Sound by Gareth Owen

COPYRIGHT INFORMATION

(See also page ii)

CHARACTERS

Frank, fifty-something
Alan, late teens

SYNOPSIS OF SCENES

ACT I   A ledge on the side of a building/An office
ACT II   An office. Three years later

Time — the present

AUTHOR'S NOTE

"No Going Back"

The song from Alan's band is something Alan should feel really comfortable singing and playing — if he can play a little guitar. Each production is hereby at liberty to write their own tune to the lyrics — ideally the actor playing Alan being involved in the process — so that he can sing along in Act I and perform live in Act II, each time with confidence and gusto.

Interruptions

A speech normally follows the one preceding it but if there is an interruption the point of interruption is marked with a /.

Eg.

Alan The paperweight / with —
Frank The paperweight off that desk?

A Word About Letters

The letters are collectively the third character in this two-hander. Part of the challenge is meeting the rather unusual stage requirement of several large, three-dimensional letters, strong enough to sit on if required. In the very first — and most rudimentary — production they were built from wood, and by bevelling some of the right-angled edges there was no need for any curves at all. The round letters (**a**, **e** and **o**) were effectively adapted squares, which then meant the **o**, for example, was easily strong enough to sit on. The tallest letter, the capital **F**, was made stable by weighting the bottom, and because the **r** and **n** were all right angles, fitting them together provided a very striking capital **S**.

One simple way of making them light up is to fake the electric cable on stage, and cover or outline the letters in a particular paint or cord (the kind used by DJs) which reacts to ultra violet light. Some u.v. tubes can then be cued, giving a very effective "flickering on" effect.

Tim Firth

For John Nutter
— a true man of letters

ACT I

A ledge perched high on the side of a building in the north of England

Between the front lip of the ledge and the back wall there is enough room to move freely about, but there's not exactly acres of space. Giving out on to the ledge is a large sliding window. Through it we can see part of an office. Over the side wall is the top of a hooped descent ladder. Off the front there is a drop of about sixty feet. The wind blows up some traffic noise and tickles a flag, now somewhat dog-eared, reading "FORSHAWS"

Into view in the office come Frank (fifty-something) and Alan (something-teen). Frank is wearing carefully-ironed blue overalls with a meticulously presented shirt and tie underneath. His leather toolbelt has nary a scratch. Alan is a slightly gauche, awkward late teen, wearing trainers, scruffy jeans and a hooded top. We don't know it yet, but he is listening to an iPod, invisible beneath his hood. They are wearing safety equipment and struggling with something we can't yet see. It's good double glazing. We can't hear a thing. The gestures coming from Frank seems to be suggest the conversation is of the ilk of "gently ... gently ... Now was that 'gently'? Was that REALLY what you'd call gently?" Etc.

They are bearing a long red object

Frank (*sliding the doors open*) ... AB-solute danger, the AB-solute life-threatening peril of what we are now about to do. So just WATCH me. Just WATCH me, OK. Just WATCH.

Frank starts to back out on to the ledge, steering in and setting down a huge red capital **F**

I stay close to the building. I do that in case there's a cross-wind, which I've judged there might be because we're up sixty feet, and it's an exposed westerly position. I've worked all that out between the vending machine and here, OK?

Alan doesn't respond

So the moment we — I tell you what we DON'T do, Alan, we don't look at the view. One strong gust you'll be IN it. You'll be half way to bloody Doncaster like Mary Poppins. Anywhere near the — (*he gestures to the floor of the ledge*) — "line of danger", we HOOK. (*He gestures to the safety equipment*) Before we look, we hook. (*He hooks Alan on to the safety rig*) Useful little ... memory ... Y'know. Mnemonic. (*He hooks himself on*) Good. And so we got her up pristine. (*He inspects the* **F**) Which is important. Has to mean as much to you as it does to Mr Forshaw that his name's up here right. Pride. Lesson one.

Alan stands, blank to the point of lobotomy. Frank turns to look out

But that's your reward. No one else gets to see the views we do, Alan. Apart from Chloe in the computer room, but that's through glass. This is elemental. Just you, the air and the bypass ... (*he nods*) ... and the folly, 'course. Up there. Fourth Lord Preston, seventeen eighty-two, built a tower on the moor. Just — no reason. Just a beautiful tower. Like his legacy for all time. (*His face clouds*) And now it's got "Becky's A Slag" sprayed all over it. I tell you, as a society, Alan, we reap what we sow, and part of a civilization dies when it starts to accept graffiti as an art form. Don't you think? It's like viewing the desecration of graves as a form of sculpture. (*He turns to Alan*) D'you think that? (*Beat*) Socially? (*Beat*) In terms of a society?

Alan just stares into the distance

I'm not going too fast, am I? Are there any questions you want to ask?

Alan sees Frank looking at him. So he pulls back his hood and takes out the earphones which he has been wearing throughout all this. They are producing a "tss tss tss" of a song

Alan Y' what?

Frank looks at him, stricken. We feel a grand canyon open up between them

Frank Give that here. I'm not recapping, Alan. I'm not going back over — *Give.*

Alan dully unplugs the player from the headphones, and gives it to Frank

You have got a real *chance* here, you know that? Doing y'r work experience someplace like this. It's not like the rest of your schoolmates, hangin' round the set of *Emmerdale* thinking they're all gonna work in telly. This is a real, proper job with a real, local firm which has been here — d'you know how long this firm's been here? On this site? Go on. Guess.

Alan doesn't look too bothered

Have a guess.

Pause

Alan Two thousand years?

Frank composes himself

Frank Today we find ourselves putting up letters on a fire escape. Question one you should be asking yourself like *THAT* — (*He clicks his fingers*) "Why"? (*He gestures out*) Answer? Proposed site of new White Rose Retail Park across bypass, thus new advertising opportunity to rear of building. Question two. "What potential problems does this location pose me as Installation Engineer"? (*He gestures*) "Risk of electrocution for escaping personnel". "Oh no". Solution? MT —

Alan yawns. It creates a frosty moment

MT-forty-seven vertical bracketing system. The princess of all bracketing systems. (*He sets off on another one*) Electrocution, Alan, is the ghost that stalks all of us in the public electrical installation industry. Safety is paramount. Safety is the *sine qua non*. Without safety we —

Alan (*touches letter and acts as though electrocuted*) DZZZZTT-AAAAAAAAAARGH.

He does this rather well and Frank leaps for the isolator

Frank JESUS LORD ABOVE, ISOLATOR! GET THE ISOL — !

Frank realises the score. Beat. Alan gives a little smile but drops it

Absolutely not funny. *Completely* not funny.

Alan goes hangdog

Complete —— (*Compose, compose*) Go and get the next letter.

Alan retreats dully towards the window. He forgets he is attached. Clunk. Alan stops, steps back, unhooks himself and goes a second time. Neither look at each other during this little moment

Alan exits

And some seed did fall on barren ground. (*He looks at his watch. He checks the coast is clear. He produces an old dictation machine that has seen long service and speaks into it*) "The defector, Ivan Bulgovsky, stared over the rooftops of lower Moscow. He tapped the balustrade of Zebschniffsky Bridge with one of his old, wizened fingers. (*Beat*) The wind had bitter teeth. Someone once said there were no mountains between here and Stowmarket in East Anglia. But oh, East Anglia seemed far away now. He closed his eyes and he were back in Cambridge, stretched on the banks of the River —— (*He can't remember it*) — of the river with a bottle of champagne in one hand and in the other a copy of Wittgenstein, signed by the author. And there, drifting towards him, was Anatevka. For a moment, there was silence but for the plop of her punt pole plopping in the water. Then softly, with the warmth of twenty summers, she whispered the offer his heart had been yearning to hear."

Alan (*off, shouting*) D'YOU WANT A TWIX, FRANK?

Frank *Forget the Twix*! Forget the flamin' — GET THE LETTERS. The government didn't set this scheme up for you to eat Twixes. (*Quickly, into the dictation machine*) "'Kiss me, Ivan,' said Anatevka. How could he know where that one kiss would lead? One kiss. One affair. One one-way ticket to Zebschniffsky Bridge." (*He clicks off. Then thinks for a moment. He clicks it back on*) Note to self. May need to come up with better name than "Anatevka". (*He clicks off. Then thinks for a moment. He clicks it back on*) Also "Zebschniffsky".

A loud glass-smash is heard off

Oh, for God's —— what was that? Alan, what ——

Frank helps Alan battle through the window ...

WATCH THE COMPUTERS! And the window ...

... and bring out a large red lower case letter **a**

What've you broken?

Alan (*with some lack of elocution*) It was a kind of snowstorm thing
th —
Frank What?
Alan The snowstorm.

Frank looks up to the skies

Frank What language are you hearing me in?
Alan The paperweight / with —
Frank The *paperweight* off that desk?
Alan It FELL off that d —
Frank (*it's the end of the world*) Oh well that's only Chloe's. She's only
been working here a month! Alan these are *my* offices, all right? These
are the people I have to work with everyday, and if —

Frank's attention is caught by the letter **a**

Little quiz. How d'you spell "Forshaws"?

Alan looks at him suspiciously

The name. This company. How d'you / spell — ?
Alan "F"...
Frank "F". Yes. Good start. Cracking start. Yes? Keep going.
Alan (*treading on coals*) "O"...
Frank Right let's just stop there, shall we? Let's just stop there and
have a chat with THIS little fella.
Alan (*pointing at the* **a**) The "O" was at the back.

Frank composes himself and goes to hook Alan back on

Frank In life, Alan, there are two kinds of people. Them who get things
in order in the depot, and them who end up sixty foot off the ground
juggling armfuls of letters and killing someone with a six foot "h".
Now what d'you want to be, eh?

Alan shrugs with a small noise

Well I tell you what you'll be if you keep doing *that*. (*He mimes Alan's
shrug and noise*) No one who shrugged ever got anywhere in life,
Alan. Presidents of the United States, Paul McCartney — "Shall we
go an' write *Hey Jude*, Paul?" (*Shrugging*) "I'm not faffed, I'm having
a cup of tea." I tell you, psychologically —
Alan Is it tea?

Frank looks at him

Is it tea?

Frank looks at him

You just said "tea".

Frank looks at him

Frank Sit down. (*He sits Alan down*) I'm going to tell you now probably
the most important lesson you'll ever get taught in the whole of your
life. (*Beat*) World's changing, Alan. All these — (*He points out over
the view like the "Boyhood Of Raleigh"*) — "White Roses", these
new retail parks. Different way of building. Thrown up overnight
practically. And Mr *Forshaw*, OK, when I asked him couple of weeks
back what that meant, like, in general, for us as a company, you know
what he said? (*Leaning in*) "As long as there is a Forshaw's on this
site, Frank Tollit will be Head of Installation."

This is clearly important to Frank

Y'know why he said that? Because thirty-five years ago a young Frank
Tollit sat like you're sitting now and he knew there were bigger things
in life than tea breaks, yes?
Alan Yeah.
Frank Yes.
Alan (*much quieter*) Lunch.
Frank (*at the flag:*) Colin Forshaw will've known since he was eighteen,
anything — *seven* that he wanted to have his name up on buildings. /
To be a ——
Alan Ymmrrhrr.
Frank (*on it like a hawk*) I'm sorry?

Alan doesn't really want to venture much further

Sorry, I missed your erudite contribution there ...?
Alan No one knows when they're seven. When I was seven I wanted
to be a fire engine.
Frank I'm not saying he knew he wanted to run a commercial lettering
factory, but *succeed*. Alan. Is what I'm saying. In here.

Pause. Yes?

Are we getting somewhere?

Pause. Alan does a "hrm" for "yes"

Go and get the next one.

Alan gets up to go. Frank softens a moment

Hey, and Alan? (*He chucks him a coin*) Have a cup of tea on me, eh?
(*He smiles paternally*)
Alan There i'n't any.
Frank What?
Alan There i'n't any left.
Frank There's a vending machine.
Alan It's gone.
Frank It was there five minutes ago.
Alan It's gone.
Frank What, it waited till we went past, then made a break for it?
Alan (*shrugging*) Idnrrmrr ...
Frank *Don't shrug.* (*Beat*) Go down to the third floor machine. By
Brian's office. That's the design department, but if there's any trouble,
tell them Frank, Head Of Installation, sent you.
Alan *You* want a cup of tea?
Frank Well I do *now*. After all that I'm thirsty *now*. But it's not a "tea
break". I want the next module up here. And a biscuit.
Alan What if that one's gone as well?
Frank It won't have gone. They're not planning a coup.

*Alan does a habitual reach for his iPod only to remember he hasn't got
it*

Alan (*gesturing "putting on earphones"*) Kanna havgrmmm?
Frank You know, contrary to modern thought human beings do not
need music in their ears to be able to move.

Alan mutters, takes off his safety hook and slopes off

Frank checks he's gone, then turns on the tape recorder

"Suddenly the Moscow night was split by a gunshot. A Gussorkski two
point five side-loaded manual ... automatic. Bulgovsky recognized it
instantly. The princess of sideloading manual automatics. He turned
to see Anatev — whatever she's — new name — standing on the

deserted bridge. Drops of her blood began to plop into the snow as red as the lips that whispered "run". Out of the patrol box emerged the large ex-KGB figure of Illyor Smirnoff. And a chase started that one way or another would last the rest of Bulgovsky's life." (*He's chuffed with that*) End paragraph. Three asterisks. (*He bops the "off" button, and starts to move the letter* **F**) Frank Tollit began writing at the age of eighteen. His early influences were John le Carré and Frederick Forsyth. (*He starts to put the* **F** *into position*) Many of his novels have been turned into successful films, starring Michael Caine. He now lives on the Roecastle Council Estate with his wife, the actress and model Jane Seymour. They have two children. Jeremy, nineteen, who is at Cambridge and opens the batting for Yorkshire ——

There is a call of annoyance, and a huge glass-smash off

Right. That's it. Out here.
Alan (*off, protesting*) I'm carrying an "o".

Alan steers through the **o** *with its cargo of a tea, a fruit drink and some biscuits*

Frank } (*together*) { Out! That is the last time. Come here. Come here.
Alan } { I'm balancing tea on an "o" an' y' can't turn corners easy 'cause the ends stick out and you have to keep it lev —— argh!

Frank steers Alan to the edge

Frank THIS is a ledge!
Alan I'm not hooked!
Frank THAT is a sixty-foot drop.
Alan I've not "hooked and looked".
Frank THAT is why hamfisted, clumsy installers ——
Alan (*suddenly*) I DON'T LIKE BEING CLUMSY.

There is a moment. Frank is slightly chastened

Don't wanna be it, do I? Don't LIKE it.

Frank doesn't quite know what to say. Alan deposits the **o**. *Frank, in the rather dodgy pause, hands back the iPod to Alan. Alan in return gives him a two-pack of digestives. For a moment it's like a hostage swap on a Moscow bridge*

Was there any trouble?

No response

D'y see anyone?

Alan shakes his head

What's this?
Alan Digestives. 'S all they had.

Frank views the Spartan biscuit with considerable disappointment. He unwraps it. He looks at it. He nibbles it. Sighs. It'll have to do. Alan produces a Twix. He unwraps it slowly and bites. Frank stops dead and stares at him

Frank Excuse me.

Alan stops dead, his mouth full. Frank looks at his digestives, then at Alan's Twix

How come the Twix Fairy didn't stop at my house?
Alan You said "biscuit".
Frank Twix IS a biscuit.
Alan (*semi-muttering*) 'Snnurssa sweet.
Frank "Twix. Smooth milk chocolate, chewy caramel on a crunchy BISCUIT base."
Alan Doesn't make it a "biscuit" just 'cause it's got "biscuit" in it ——
Frank So what's it make it?
Alan (*quieter*) Well it ——
Frank A caravan? Come on? A risotto?
Alan Look ——
Frank No, you carry on, mate. You carry on with your Twix. I'll just tuck into my double-whipped cream flake flaming plain digestive. (*He disdainfully takes a mouthful*)
Alan (*quietly*) Mrrrgrmmoo said digestives.
Frank (*like a hawk*) I did NOT say "digestives". I said "biscuit".
Alan (*with a weary sigh*) "Biscuit", / I mean.
Frank I happen to know I would never say "digestive", because I tend to use the word "McVitie's" or "Homewheat".
Alan Mrrgrmm.

Pause

Frank I mean, it's just a little thing here, Alan, but we do have sometimes to remember in life, who is the YTS trainee ——

Alan (*under*) "YTS"?

Frank — and who is the Head of Installation ——

Alan What's YTS?

Frank The overall head of all installation in this company giving out thirty-five years of experience all neatly packaged up ——

Alan D'you want a Twix?

Frank — all free. And little things like "who gets Twixes or digestives" — doesn't matter to *me* ——

Alan Do you want a Twix?

Frank — *I* don't mind. But there's other people in life, I have to warn you, who ——

Alan (*loudly*) Look have a flaming Twix. Go on, have eight. (*He produces an enormous number of Twixes*)

Frank is momentarily speechless

Frank Where d'you get them all from?

Alan The machine. They were giving 'em away.

Frank And here's me putting fifty p in every time and there's a button that gives them away.

Alan Blokes were giving them out.

Frank People don't give away Twixes, Alan.

Alan They / *were* ——

Frank The day they start giving away Twixes the ravens'll leave the Tower of London.

Alan Look ——

Frank "First signs of the apocalypse. The mountains sink, the seas boil and folk start handing out Twixes."

Alan (*louder to shut him up*) The blokes did it who were taking the machine away.

Pause

Frank What, permanently?

Alan I don't know, do I? I don't work here.

Frank registers this as odd. He eats his biscuit

Frank Must be a problem with them all.

Pause

Alan D'you always do that?
Frank What?
Alan Going on — (*waving loosely*) Taking a sentence then going on an' on about it.

Frank gives him a look

The ravens. Then all that after it. About Twixes and the seas boiling.
Frank (*studiedly*) The ravens "re." the Twix is called a "metaphor". Going "on and on about it" is called an "extended metaphor".
Alan D'you know all about that?
Frank 'Course I "know al —— " I'm a writer. I have to. It'd be like a gardener not knowing what his roses were called. It'd be like a mechanic / not...
Alan See, you're doing it again.
Frank Yes. Well. It's instinct, isn't it. Writer's instinct.
Alan What're you doing up here if you're a writer? I'n't it a bit hard keeping y'r paper flat?
Frank (*killing him with a little laugh*) Obviously I don't *write* up here. I use moments at work to — harvest my thoughts. Then I go home and write 'em up.
Alan You written anythin' famous?
Frank (*slightly on glass*) Depends what you mean by "famous".
Alan That you can buy in railway stations.

Frank hedges slightly

Frank I have had stuff sold in railway stations, yes. D'you know *The Yorkshireman*?
Alan Is it a thriller?
Frank It's a *magazine*. About Yorkshire.
Alan Oh, right, yeah. The little one that's all about moles and dry stone walling.
Frank It's not all about that. It's got the highest circulation of any regional magazine in the north of England.
Alan Mostly people interested in moles / who ——
Frank It's not peop—— it's *everyone* who buys it. Doctors buy it. Dentists have it lying round in — in — in — It's a kaleidoscope of Yorkshire life. (*Pause*) And I've had stuff ... (*He nods meaning "in there"*)
Alan Story?
Frank Article.

Alan About what?

Frank (*after a pause*) My childhood in Batley. (*Quickly*) But I write spy
stories primarily. Espionage.

Alan Oh aye. Like thrillers? I like them. The big thick ones?

Frank Thickness isn't the prime consideration ——

Alan But they are thick. That's why they sell 'em in rail stations. So
they take up the whole journey.

Frank (*patiently*) As I say, thickness / isn't ——

Alan Although sometimes it's a con, because it looks thicker, but the
typeset's bigger, so on the page you get less novel per square inch.

Frank didn't expect Alan to know a word like "typeset"

'Cause sometimes they do it in massive fonts. And nobody notices
'cause they all think books come in the same font, but if you put some
next to each other, some are bigger and some have got little serifs on
the "a"s and the "t"s that take up space and some have normal letter
"g"s, and some still have that weird little two-circles-on-top-of-each-
other thing that looks like a duck staring upwards. (*He eats some more
Twix*)

Frank coughs to prepare the ground

Frank Yeah well I, er ... I've written three. Novels. All with potential
for television, you know. Television spy dramas.

Alan Have they been on?

Frank cools

Frank Well, they're in various — (*he nods a "you know"*) I sent one to
the BBC in Leeds who wrote me a really sweet letter saying although
they'd love to do spy thrillers, they only had the budget for local news
and weather and they'd send it on to the BBC in London. That's where
it is now.

Alan whistles dully in appreciation

It's called *The Spy Who Went Out In The Warm*. (*Pause*) Can you see
what I'm doing with that? *The Spy Who Came In From The Cold*?
It's like a tongue in cheek little — clever little — y'know. Clever
twist. (*Beat*) It was going to be *The Spy Without A Jumper*, which was
even cleverer, where you have to — y'know — (*He gestures at "make*

the —— ") — *deduce*. But you can't have the word "jumper" in a title.
It's one of those words you can't use. Like "casserole".
Alan Right.
Frank Y'see that's writer-instinct kicking in. It's like *Ice Cold In Alex*.
It's hard. It's direct. It's a good title. But like "Freezing In Alex". Not
as good. "Bit Nippy In Alex" ——
Alan You couldn't call it "Bit Nippy / In —— "
Frank No that's what I'm saying, / it's ——
Alan You wanna call it something like *The Vatican Inheritance*. 'Cause
that's a good title 'cause that immediately makes you think, y' know
... y' know.. "What IS ... that?" "What CAN someone inherit from a
Vatican?" Have you read that one?

Beat

Frank I think I started it.
Alan Ah God y' can't STOP with that one! How it keeps twistin'. How
you think you've sussed out who's watchin' him, and it's wrong. And
you think it's someone else and then THAT'S wrong. And you keep
going ... (*he gestures*) ... bam-bam-bam-bam, getting it wrong 'til he
gets rescued at the end in the sand dunes! GOD that's great, that is.
THAT's what keeps you reading on trains, in't it? When it keeps being
unexpected. Who's it wrote that?
Frank I think it was Anthony Bel / gravia ——
Alan Belgravia. That's it. (*In wonder*) "Anthony Belgravia. The Vatican
Inheritance." (*Beat*) Best *ever* ——
Frank (*suddenly*) Anyway. Come on.
Alan You can lend it you if want.
Frank "Lending" is a transitive verb, Alan. If I were to "lend" it then
technically I'd be giving it to you.

Frank whistles Alan out like a sheepdog

Alan I haven't finished me / tea ——
Frank Mr Forshaw wants these lit up at five thirt —— We don't have
tea breaks, I told you. One "r", please, and one "s". And don't knock
anything. Lesson two.

Alan unhooks and disappears behind the glass

Alan (*as he departs*) Hrrrmmrr.

Frank thinks a moment. He presses the dictation machine

Frank "Bulgovsky raced out on to the sloping roof of the — Kremlin. With each movement his boots scooped up more and more snow, slowing him down. Smirnoff was gaining until he was within touching distance of Bulgovsky's ankle. Suddenly Bulgovksy's hand was clasped. He looked up with thankful eyes through the snow to see that *there* — (*beat*) ... unexpectedly ... reaching out to him ... totally unexpectedly, on the roof of the Kremlin ... (*beat*) ... was Neil Diamond. Singing *Sweet Caroline*."
Alan (*off*) Hey, Frank!

Alan appears behind the window with an **r** *and an* **n**

There's no "s". I got the "r", but there's no "s" down — whoa!
Frank Mind the computers! Twenty grand of computers, those are.
Alan There's no "s" down there anywhere.
Frank There must be an "s" / down ——
Alan So I did what you said an' brought the next one up, like "ready". Only thing is, it's not an "h". It's an "n".

Frank looks at them

Frank Where have you been getting these?
Alan "Assembled materials despatch".
Frank Which pile?
Alan There's only one pile left.

Frank decides something, then unhooks and pushes past Alan

Frank Get these bolted to that MT-forty-seven.
Alan On me own?
Frank Princess of bracketing sys —— yes, on your own. It's your first job. You should be proud. I was proud on my first job.

Frank disappears

Alan watches him go. He sees Frank's tape recorder. He inspects it with some amusement. He presses "review" and hears:

Frank's Voice (*on the machine*) You should be proud. I was proud on my first job.

Click. Alan finds this amusing

Alan (*mimicking*) "I was proud on my first job". It was the Spring of sixteen forty-eight ...

*Alan has an idea. He puts the iPod by the dictation machine and seems quickly to find a way to plug the two together. It plays a track! It's quite a palatable guitar riff intro. Alan stands on the **n** like a rock star at Live Aid*

ARE YOU WATCHING, BATLEY-Y! (*To represent "the crowd responding"*) Waa-aaaaa! Gonna start with one you might recognize. (*He nods, cockily*) This is "NO GOING BACK". (*To represent "the crowd responding"*) Waa-aaaaa.

*Alan starts to sing along the words as he puts up the **F***

> You made your bed now it needs lying in
> You put your chips all down on black
> You burnt the bridges on your Rubicon
> And now — there's no going back.

*Frank appears behind the window, aghast. He deposits an **l** and ploughs out with an **r***

You chose your exit off the motorway ——
Frank Oi! *Oi!*

Alan quickly swipes off the machine and has it swiped off him by Frank

Get that off! *Get that —— ! Stop it!*
Alan It won't've erased anything.
Frank Give it here! (*He checks the machine*)
Alan You wanna get one of these. Save you carrying half a brick around.
Frank (*holding up his dictation machine*) Has mine got a "record" button?
Alan Well yes / but ——
Frank Does it "record" things?
Alan We've got two / "r"s.
Frank (*snapping*) *I know we've got two "r"s.* I've just found that out, haven't I? I've just brought the bugger up here. I don't need you to tell me we've got two "r"s.

*Alan looks at it. He deposits the **r***

Alan Should we check the plans?

Frank turns, affronted

Frank I'm *sorry*?
Alan Probably be on the computers somewhere. (*Nervous beat*) If
there's ... (*with more trepidation*) ... "twenty thousand pounds of
compute —— "
Frank (*deathly*) The words "Head Of Installation" all have capitals,
Alan. You know what those three capitals together signify?
Alan (*doing it in his head*) "HOI"?
Frank That it's a *position*.
Alan (*quietly*) Oh right.
Frank That is *achieved*. After thirty-five *years*. And after thirty-five
years of experience you do NOT need a plan to erect the word
"Forshaw".
Alan Right ...
Frank "Equatorial Guatemalan Molasses Limited", maybe. But not my
own boss's —— (*He winces*) *Dammit.*

Alan senses the mood

Alan (*gingerly*) 'S'not actually *your* fault if ——
Frank It's always your fault. Lesson three. It's not the backroom boys,
it's not Brian in design with his bloody rectangular spectacles who
cops it.
Alan But / it ——
Frank It's US, hanging round up here with everyone going — (*He
mimics*) "God, can't put letters up in the right order. Bloody hell,
I could do that". And it's *not true*. It's a skilled job, this. I mean
you try wafting about with a bloody "seventy-eight" on the side of
"Toys 'R' Us" in a force six. You try putting an "IKEA" up when
each F-two comes in three sections an' each section's the size of
Denmark.
Alan (*"calm down"*) *All* right.
Frank THREE.
Alan All right!

Frank tries to cool it

Frank This is exactly what he wants. Get us rattled.
Alan Who?

Frank *Three weeks* he took. Three *weeks* to design "Northern Fisheries". I told him "Michaelangelo did half the bloody Sistine in that and all you've done is make the second "i" of "fisheries" into a trout.'

Alan Is this Brian —— ?

Frank I told him, "Designing's the donkey work, mate. Getting them up there, that's the art."

Alan (*pointing back inside*) — "Brian" by the vending machine?

Frank See what *this* is, this'll be his little, little ... (*he does a little "nibbling away" gesture*) ... nim-nim-nim.

Alan Him who does all the design?

Frank That's the kind of man he is, you see. With his bloody little Audi. And his *ties*. His comedy bloody — (*he points*) — there is never, Alan, in life, ANY justification for a tie that has jokes on. No one who was ever funny *ever* wore a comedy t —— a comedy tie denotes someone who wants to BE funny rather than someone who IS. Lesson four. A comedy tie always has an ulterior motive.

Alan looks out at the view

"Lit up by five o' clock, Frank". "No problem Mr Forshaw." It'll be lit up all right. The word "Fronra".

Beat

Alan Sounds like one of your book titles. (*Beat*) "Ulterior Motive". (*Beat*) Y'd've had a gun and a playing card an' a couple of tickets to Moscow.

Alan starts putting the o *and the* r *into position, cabling up*

Frank What about Moscow?

Alan Y'd have had them. Cover of old spy books. Used to have these little still lifes didn't they? Dead funny. Things like a Martini an' a knife an' a couple of playing cards.

He smiles as he struggles with the letters o *and* r *into position. The "name" now reads:*

Fo —— a

A lizard, some bullets and a pair of opera glasses. (*Beat*) S'pose so people'd think "hmm, why did that lizard have a gun and why was he at the ballet?" (*Beat*) Buy the book. (*Beat*) Find out. (*He resumes work*) Do look good, though, lizards. Got a lizard on my cover.

Frank puts the r *into position. The name now reads:*

For—a

Frank You haven't had a cover. What cover?
Alan Me band. We did a CD. (*He produces a CD box from his jacket and gives it to Frank*)

Frank scowls

Alan Name of the band. "Lizard". So I drew a lizard.
Frank You drew that?
Alan Went to the zoo to get the heads right. That's not the best bit. Watch this. (*He takes it, and unfolds it out to the size of a small poster*) Lyrics to all the songs, OK? Plus drawings of like the other guys in the band, caricatures, plus drawings of their instruments ... but if I move back ... (*He walks backwards away from Frank, holding it up*) ... keep moving back ...
Frank What?
Alan Just let your eyes kind of "see" rather than "look"...

There's a beat as Frank does just that

Frank (*quietly*) Lizard.
Alan (*beaming*) Like Picasso used to do stuff where it wasn't a "face", but lots of angles of a face all like vibin' off each other. Me art teacher said it was like "controlled anarchy" and I thought — "aye aye, that's kind of what our music's like". (*He gestures — "so that's that"*) Did it like Picasso.

Alan puts it away

Bet I used the same design software as on them computers ——
Frank (*as a warning shot*) Alan ——
Alan (*able to see what's coming*) Absolutely.
Frank (*dully*) I have ——
Alan (*putting his hands up*) "Twenty-five years experience ..."
Frank All I need is two "s"s, an "h" and a "w".
Alan Well you have got one "s". (*Beat*) If you look at it one way. (*He turns the* n *on to its side*) That could be what the second "r" is for. (*He looks underneath the* r) Yeah, 's got a bolt. See? (*He fits the* r *on to the top of the* n. *It makes a capital* S) Houston, we have an "S"!

The letters now read:

For—aS

A beat of wonder

Frank "Texan Haulage".
Alan Mm?
Frank He's only gone and done a "Texan Haulage" on me, hasn't he?
  Capital at the beginning and at the end.

Frank stares at Alan. That was bright

> And that, ladies and gentlemen is what, in the rectangular eyes of
> Brian, passes for "design".

Frank reacts with a sense of victory

> *Got him! Good*, Alan. Get these on the frame.

They busy themselves cabling up

> He thinks he's outwitted us. But *we*, you and me, the lads in the front
> line ... He does a voice, y'know? When he talks to me. He goes — (*In
> a pointed northern accent*) "'Appen, Frank. 'Ow's your whippet?"

Alan (*genuinely interested*) Y've got a whippet?
Frank No it's heightened I mean. He's doing a stereotype. He's making
  a *joke*.
Alan (*pointing*) "Comedy tie".
Frank (*pointing back*) "Ulterior motive".
Alan Hockey stick, two cyanide capsules and a dead hamster.
Frank How's someone your age —— ? Did you have these books lying
  round at home?

Alan snorts a slight rueful laugh to the contrary

> No?

Alan Only books in our house are car manuals.
Frank (*taking this in*) Book a week, me dad always said. Still does.
  Down the library. Keeps your mind alive to imagination an' fantasy /
  and the whole ——
Alan Oh I don't like *them* books.
Frank What books?

Alan You know. Where things happen that y' think ... "that wouldn't happen".

Frank "Things happening that wouldn't happen" is broadly what we call fiction.

Alan *Vatican Inheritance* was in the fiction bit an' there's nothing in *that* that wouldn't happen.

Frank No but I'm talking about — *wonder*. The whole world of ... of ...

Frank detects a "nrrr" of dismissal from Alan

You can't — (*he does it*) — "nrrr" about wonder, Alan.

Alan works on, but Frank's not going to let it drop

D'you not wonder about anything in life? D'y' not sit there sometimes and look at the world and ——

Alan There is one thing I wonder about.

Frank (*leaping on it*) Well there you go, see ——

Alan Y'r on a train to Leeds. (*Beat*) Y've gone to the buffet car for a diet coke. And you have one person in each of the joining bits between the carriages ready to press the buttons that make the doors open on a given command. If you shouted "now", and they all pressed, and the doors all opened and you jumped in the air, why don't you end up at the back of the train?

Pause. Frank looks at him

Frank Well, it's ... (*He gestures loosely*) … pressure isn't it? Air pressure. It's ... it's ...

Pause. Frank needs a full stop

Different.

That's it

Alan (*after a pause, nodding*) Right. Ta.

Alan mouth-shrugs, resumes and brings out the **l**

Frank Is that it? Have I just answered the only question you had in life?

Alan (*smiling*) You like saying that, don't you?

Frank frowns a "what"?

"In life". You "in life" all the time. Everything's "in life ..."
something.
Frank Do I?
Alan Sounds like there should be a list of 'em. "In life..." by Frank.
Perhaps that should be your next book. (*He raises the* l) Got the first
bit of the "h".

Frank evaluates this. The lad doesn't miss much. He points where the l
should go

Frank Are y' gonna do art at college, then?

Alan screws up his nose to suggest the negative

Should show 'em that lizard.
Alan (*not pausing*) I did.
Frank College?
Alan Showed 'em lots of things. They had the whole folder.
Frank (*reading the situation*) Oh. I see. Well. (*He looks out*) Y' could
try again next year, y'know? Some years, if they haven't had you first
time, things change and ——
Alan They would've had me first time. (*Re. the* l) This going here? (*He
positions the* l)
Frank What d'you say?
Alan Come on. (*He does a "Frank"*) "Government didn't set this
scheme up to eat Twixes."

The letters now read:

For–l–a–S

Frank You turned down college?
Alan (*with a slight smile*) It wasn't "college" college. It wasn't bloody
— mortar boards. It was an art vocational thing at Batley Tech.
Frank What the hell difference does that make?
Alan Sorry. "University Of West Yorkshire".
Frank Why d'you turn it down?

Alan shrugs and does a noise

Don't do that.

Alan God, d'you always get the inquisition when you put up letters?

Frank That lizard's all right.

Alan Yeah. Well there you go. I didn't go to college to do that, did I? I went to the zoo.

Frank Alan. Do not make the mistake of thinking college is about learning. College is about "meeting".

Alan Frank ——

Frank The meeting of the people who get your drawings on the front of books. 'Cause y' won't, I'm telling y'. Without college. You're up against that lot who come out from Cambridge.

Alan Anyway ——

Frank They bloody churn 'em out. All these rows of shiny-faced graduates who all look like Sebastian Coe. That's who you're up against.

Alan I'm not up against them. I'm up here with you.

Frank Do you not want your stuff on the front of books?

Alan Be all right if it happened.

Frank And what makes it "happen"? The Happen Fairy comes down and sprinkles some "Happen Dust" around / and ——

Alan You like fairies as well, don't you?

Frank So you ——

Alan We've had the Twix Fairy ——

Frank — you turn down college an' what?

Alan Now it's the Happen Fairy ...

Frank You stand about doing nothing ...

Alan *Frank.*

Frank What?

Alan I enjoy meself, all right?

Frank Putting up letters on a business unit in Batley?

Alan (*sharply*) I thought you were proud of it.

Pause. Frank's gaze swings away

Frank (*on auto pilot*) Bring up everything that's left.

Alan (*after a beat*) There's only an "e". (*Pause*) Under / the ——

Frank I *am* proud of it. But I've got me writing as well, haven't I? Changes everything, that does. When stuff goes in *The Yorkshireman*, and it's there in railway stations, it's just — you can't describe that, Alan. It's like cold fountains going off inside y'.

Beat. Traffic passes

Frank At the front there's only an "e", but there's more at the back.

Alan Broken.

Frank Under the tarpaulin.

Alan They're all broken.
Frank No, they *look* broken, but actually they're FD-threes which /
   are —
Alan Frank they were in bits and the ends were splintered. The only
   complete letter left down there is an old lower case "k" designed to
   look like three french sticks.

Pause

   We could look on a computer.

Pause

Frank Or we could retain our dignity and wait till Chloe gets back off
   lunch.

He sits pointedly. Alan looks out at the view, slightly pained

Alan Frank. It's rush hour. I don't think she's going to be at lunch, is she?

Frank looks at his watch. It is

   I don't think she's coming back.

*Frank is faced with a brick wall. This is true. No way out. He grits his
teeth. And grabs his jacket*

   What are you doing?
Frank If that's what he wants.
Alan Who?
Frank That's what all this is, y' see? All another little "how's your
   whippet?". Some people do this, Alan. This is how some people will
   operate in life. I have to warn you. And what you have to remember is
   the Colin *Forshaws* ... (*he gestures to the flag*) ... never taken in by all
   that. Lesson five. Good guys respect good guys. And your "Brians",
   what bloody burns them up is knowin' there's people out there like
   you who can do all that with that lizard, and all they'll ever be able to
   do is make the "k" of "bakery" look like three french sticks.

Frank goes out

*Once he's sure Frank has gone, Alan nips in to the office, grabs a laptop
off a desk and taps in the way someone does when they know exactly
what they're doing*

Alan (*"of course"*) Oh *God-d!* (*Louder*) Frank?

No answer, so Alan doesn't wait. He dumps the laptop, moves the **l***, then the* **S***. The letters now read:*

For Sal

At that second, like a spectre, Frank appears in the office with a lower case **e**

All right, Frank?

Frank's whole mien has changed

I was er ... (*He nods inside*) — cleaning the snowstorm up, I knocked
the computer. It came on and ...
Frank (*quietly*) Bit of help?

Alan starts to heave the **e** *up to the end. It now reads, quite clearly:*

For Sale

Alan Did Brian tell you?
Frank (*after a beat*) Get her cabled up.
Alan (*cheerfully*) Should've seen it coming, eh? New retail parks. All
gonna need letters. Company making 'em's gonna need bigger ——

Frank hands him a letter

— bigger factory, isn't it? (*Reading*) Aye aye? "Memo to Brian, head
of design". Been doing a bit of espionage?! (*Reading*) "Re. company
relocation. The ...."

He tails off. Frank does it for him

Frank "The company relocation conference will take place the afternoon
of Friday, the fourteenth."

Alan checks the date on his watch. Yup. That's today

I bought this book on writing once. "How To". "For Dummies", kind
of thing. Said the art is making the reader fill in what you don't tell
them. (*Beat*) Would we agree what that letter tells us, by not telling us,
is that the Relocation Fairy hasn't stopped at my house?

Alan has no answer. What can he say? Frank breathes in to summon energy

P-Nines. (*He points at an isolator box on one of the letters*) Electrical isolators. Situated on the rear of each letter.

Alan Aren't you going to do anything?

Frank Devil's own thing to fit ...

Alan You're putting yourself out of a job.

Frank In fact a lot a people can't be faffed, which ——

Alan Doing your job is putting yourself out of one.

Frank — leaves the public exposed to electrocution.

Alan That's like a dry-stone waller smashing himself over the head with a rock.

Frank First, take a very small flat-head screwdriver.

Alan No.

Frank Alan, we've been given the brief / and ——

Alan (*matching it*) Don't start givin' me all that old trouper rubbish.

Frank Alan, in life / there ——

Alan And don't bloody "in life" — I'm fed up of being "in life"-d. Why don't you try "in life"-ing yourself. Lesson seven.

Frank "As long as there's a Forshaw's on this site, Frank Tollit will be Head Of Installation." Hey, I tell y' what, eh? (*He is drawn towards the drop*) Makin' people fill in what he hasn't told 'em. Very clever. (*After a slight pause*) 'Specially if it's easier for them to fill in than it is for you to say.

Alan stands, worried

Alan Tell you what we don't do, Frank. We don't look at the view. (*He doesn't know what Frank is intending to do*) You've looked but y've not hooked.

Frank What are you doing here, Alan?

Alan (*after a pause*) I was too late applyin' for *Emmerdale*.

Frank doesn't respond

You're not going to jump off, are you? (*Pause*) It's just I wouldn't have anyone to fill in me assessment form.

This causes half a smile

Frank You can draw.

Alan Yeah, an' you can write. And that's / a ledge ——

Frank No, no, no. You see, that's the thing. (*Beat*) I *want* to write. But
I have this problem, you see, Alan. I have this problem. An' you see,
the problem is — (*beat*) I'm crap.

Alan doesn't know what to say to this

I didn't ask for it. I didn't ASK to want to write. But when God sat
up there and gave me this terrible burning ... (*he searches for words*)
... *burn* to see my name up in railway stations — and he did, Alan,
Christ — when he gave me that, he said, "Here you go, Frank. And
just to make it a little more interesting, I'll give you the ambition, but
absolutely no talent. Absolutely bugger all". (*Pause*) And then he sat
back and he laughed himself stupid.

Alan You've had stuff published.

Frank Oh I have, yes. In *The Yorkshireman*. You know what it was about?

Alan Your childhood in Batley.

Frank No. Moles. You were right first time. I lied.

Alan Look, / I didn't mean ——

Frank When I write about any other kind — like spy "moles", what
happens is Bulgovsky, you see, he climbs up this roof in Moscow, and
gets pulled to safety by Harry Dubjeck. Who grabs him, brings him up
real close and says "Hold on. You're just a poor version of me."

Alan Who's Harry Dubjeck?

Frank (*after a beat*) Thought y'd read *The Vatican Inheritance*.

Alan (*after a slight pause: "Oh, right"*) Well maybe he is *now* but if
y' try again. Y' keep going — I bet — God, how old was Anthony
Belgravia before he started writing anything decent?

Frank Twelve. (*Beat*) Maybe eleven, if you count the pretend newspaper
reports he used to write of our football matches.

Pause. Alan frowns. What?

The back garden of twenty-four, Fontainebleu Road, Batley. Great
garden that was. For football. Beech tree and a pear.

Alan You *knew* Anthony Belgravia?

Beat

Frank I knew Tony Bell. And I tell y', I knew that Tony Bell was
going to turn into "Anthony Belgravia" just from reading his made-up
newspaper. I could tell. (*Beat*) Maybe that's one thing I CAN do.

Alan Have y' never spoke?

Frank "Spoke-*n*". (*He looks out*) I did think about sending him a copy
of *The Yorkshireman*. To show I'd had something published. (*He half*

laughs) That would've been good, eh? He's had Sean Connery in a film of his book, and I came THAT close to sending him an article on traditional mole repellents.

Beat

Alan Maybe he's got mole trouble.

Frank (*after a beat*) I don't think they have moles in Capri. Where he lives now. Married to an actress. (*After a pause*) He did fly in once. To do a book signing. (*He waves, loosely*) *Evening Gazette* made a big splash, with him being a local lad, y'know. And it just being made into a film. Borrowed some letters from us, put 'em up like ... (*He gestures*) "Hollywood" — y'know? (*Slight pause. He looks out*) And he was sat in front. An' I was up the ladder putting his name up. And I felt so far away from it all, Alan. So bloody far away.

Alan Why didn't you say hello?

Beat

Frank Same reason I never finished his *Vatican Inheritance*. (*Beat*) Sometimes it gets very hard for us Brians to face the fact that there are you Alans about.

Beat

Alan Yeah well. Bet he couldn't write a book about Batley as good as you.

Frank looks at him. He smiles

What?

Frank Y'know something, Alan. I wish I was you.

Alan finds a vague smile

Alan Now don't put THAT in a book 'cause THAT would never happen. (*Beat*) Ask me dad. He wishes I was him.

Frank You really don't care if no one sees your drawing, do you? If they're never up in a railway station?

Beat

Alan What d'you want, Frank? (*Slight pause*) In life?

Beat

Frank To be immortal. (*A slight pause*) Not for ever. Just for a bit. Just
— like old Lord Preston up there. With his folly.

Alan follows his look

You can still see him. All the cars on the bypass, they're all gonna see
him tonight. Even if they don't know who he was.

Frank stares out, deep in thought. Something galvanizes in Alan

Alan Frank will you do something for me?

Frank keeps staring out, deep in thought

Will you let me finish it off? Cable these up. Will you go and stand,
y'know ... (*He nods out to*) Building site. Tell me what it looks like?
(*Pause. He does a "Frank"*) With it being me first job. (*He smiles*) I
want to be proud of it.

*Frank turns and looks at Alan. He hands him the small flat head
screwdriver*

Frank Lesson one.

*And with that, Frank walks through the window and out of Forshaws
for the last time*

*Alan watches him go. Then he turns on his iPod. The music picks up
to fill the house with "No Going Back" as with a burst of energy, and
feverish determination he moves the letters*

The letters now read:

Fora–Ire

Starting to half sing along, he puts the **n** *after the* **a**

*Then he nips round the back and plugs in what we think are the
remaining letters*

Finally he bobs back, stands and blinks into the western sky

Alan   OK. (*Pant, pant, then shouting*) *ARE YOU WATCHING, BATLEY?*

*The letters light up. He hadn't connected the **o** or the **e** so they read*

F ranlr

Alan pushes the second **r** *back at an angle against the* **l** *to form a crude* **k**

   He exits

The neon sign over the Batley skyline tonight reads:

F rank

Black-out

Hold those letters burning out Frank's immortality. Just for a bit

CURTAIN

ACT II

An office. Three years later, late afternoon

Large windows give out on to afternoon sky and the rear of a huge bright orange capital **O C** *and* **K**. *In the opposite corner is a small hill of rejection — many boxes of electrical goods, all returned faulty, and with incriminating crosses denoting their shame. The desk is cheap to the point of insult, the office chair probably came free with an order of photocopier paper. On one wall is a poster of a band who obviously once did a gig at a pub somewhere. A band called "Lizard". In a corner with the returned goods is a beaten-up acoustic guitar case. All in all it looks like a cross between a store cupboard and a teenager's bedroom*

There is a knock at the door. No response from the returned goods

Frank (*behind the door*) Mr Grey? (*Pause. He knocks louder*) Mr Grey?

Frank enters, dressed in his smartest jacket, neatly-ironed tie, carrying a lunchbox and a clipboard

Mr Grey. Sorry. Frank Tollit.

Frank looks like he's here on some kind of inspection. He looks round. Suddenly one of the letters flickers. It catches Frank's eye

Whoa hello? (*He is drawn to it*) GOD almighty look at you.

Seeing as there's no one around, Frank slides opens the window and goes out to inspect the letters at close quarter, clearly unimpressed with the standard of workmanship

Almost immediately, a dully-dressed young businessman struggles through the door with a pad of paper, an easel and marker pens

It's Alan, three years older. He dumps his cargo, talking into a walkie-talkie. He wears a nametag

Alan Judith this is Alan. (*He notices the open window, and cursorily shuts it*) Yes I'm up in my office working on ——

There is some squawk of a woman on the other end telling him to wait

(*Grimly, after a beat*) Yes I'll wait. (*He goes to put the paper on the easel*)

The phone squawks again. Alan darts to answer it

(*Into the walkie-talkie*) Hi? Yeah, I'm up in my office working on tonight's Ten At Ten presentation so if anyone wants me, I —

As a squawk of disappointment comes at the other end, Frank appears at the window to find it shut

Yes I am "gonna be doing it". In fact could you tell everyone? Ten minutes after closing tonight I'll be doing a short, ten minute —

Frank knocks on the window

BLOODY HELL. What the — ? (*Into the walkie-talkie*) Hold on.

Alan opens the window to a flood of apologies from Frank

Frank ⎱ (*together*) ⎰ Sorry sorry sorry. I was just looking
　　　　　　　　　　　　　 at your brackets and —
Alan ⎰　　　　 ⎱ What the hell are you — ? My what?

Frank Your bracketing system. Looking at. I was looking at ...

Frank recognizes this dully-dressed drone as Alan instantly. Alan doesn't even clock Frank

Alan My b — ? Oh Right. Yeah. Sorry. Forgot one of the letters had gone out. Carry on. (*Into the walkie-talkie*) So Judith if you could ...? Judith? (*She's gone. To save face:*) OK, thank you. (*To Frank, cursorily*) Just carry on, mate. Whatever you need.

Alan starts to erect the easel. Frank awaits his moment

Frank (*pointedly*) Seems strange, being back in this building after all this time.
Alan (*not interested, "yeah?"*) Mm?
Frank (*trying again*) Few years back a young lad wrote my name on here.

Alan (*idly, whilst busy*) I know. Little hoodie bastards. See, what gets
   me, right ... It's *illegal*, right? To do graffiti? Who's selling them the
   spray cans? In the shop do they not think, "hmm ... twelve-year-old,
   hooded top, wants four shades of green, two purples and a yellow.
   Chances are he's not gonna be touching up a Mazda".
Frank No no I *knew* the lad who did it.
Alan Oh well you would of course 'cause that's the *other* thing, 'cause
   they *sign* 'em now. It's *art* now.
Frank Played in a band called "Lizard".

Alan stops dead

   Bloody awful racket but the cover was good.

Pause. Only now does Alan turn and look. REALLY look

   Lifetime for you, isn't it, three years? Who am I? Go on. Have a go.
   (*He nods*) Guess.
Alan (*slowly pointing at Frank as if the name is emerging from mist*)
   For Sale.

Frank smiles

Frank I'm the man who was "for sale".
Alan (*quietly*) It's never Frank.
Frank It's "not" Frank. "Never" implies something being "not" on a
   continuous basis.
Alan It bloody IS Frank, isn't it.
Frank And you didn't recognize. But that's what happens, y'see Alan. I
   have to warn y'. When you get to be an older man, gradually the lights
   in the word "man" start to go out 'til all you're left with is the "older".
   The "man" disappears completely. (*Beat*) Y' walk in a room, people
   just see six foot of "old" with a tie on.
Alan (*after a beat*) I was only thinking the other week, looking out
   that window, I was thinking, "Thank God old Frank's not here to see
   this".
Frank You were never thinking of me.
Alan The other night! Stood here, looking out. The whole of the White
   Rose Park — there were *three*. Only *three* store signs fully working.
   (*He points to one:*) Boots?
Frank Oh yes. "Bots".
Alan "Bots". Second time that "o"'s blown since Easter. (*He points*)
   "Tarbucks".

Frank "Obit Electrical". That should be "Orbit".
Alan (*pointing*) "Wold Of Lather".
Frank See, it's just contractors who do 'em now. Lettering's just part of the overall build.
Alan (*shaking his head*) "Obit".
Frank (*smiling*) Good job you didn't take that training seriously. Talk about a dying art.
Alan I did!
Frank In retrospect it was like training someone to do wattle and daub.
Alan I DID take it seriously.

Frank gives him a wry look

Frank Whatever, if you *had*, you'd never've ended up here, few years later, as ... (*He looks on the door*) "Small Returned Goods."
Alan Actually that sign's comin' off, that. We haven't changed that yet.
Frank Oh / right.
Alan On the door. "Returned goods" is across the corridor now.
Frank Right.
Alan They're clearing this out for my office.
Frank "Your —— " No!

Alan puts his arms out over his "kingdom"

Alan Trainee Assistant Deputy Manager.
Frank (*trying to follow that*) "Deputy — Assistant."
Alan Absolutely. (*Beat*) Is what I'm training for.
Frank Well how about that.
Alan Oh eh but it must be sweet for you, eh? This? Coming back here? Sticking it back up — what was your old place?
Frank Forshaws?
Alan Yeah-h, them old sods. Being an inspector. Giving all their letters a big "fail"?
Frank Oh sorry, when I said — (*He points outside*) The "inspecting" was just professional interest. I'm not — I'm here to meet the manager.
Alan (*frowning*) Mr Green?
Frank *Green*! Got it in me head it was Grey. I knew it was a colour. I said to meself "the manager's a colour —— "
Alan Why're you seeing Bernard?
Frank Well I have to. My assessment form's got to be signed by a manager. (*Beat*) It IS Mr Green? The manager?

Alan stares at him a beat

Yes. (*Beat*) I think ... "Second Chance" it's called. (*Beat*) Giving the
long-term unemployed a er ... (*Beat*)

Alan is suddenly acutely embarrassed

Alan Thing is, Frank, Mr Green isn't in today / and ——
Frank It's the twenty-second.
Alan (*checking his watch*) Yes, it's ——
Frank The two-ten shift?
Alan Yes but ——
Frank I remembered definitely, "twenty-two, two ten"..
Alan ⎱ (*together*) ⎰ Yeah, I ——
Frank ⎰   ⎱ ...'cause for electrical superstores it's the
                        quietest time ...
Alan ⎱ (*together*) ⎰ It's ——
Frank ⎰   ⎱ ... shops selling televisions and fridges and ——
Alan I know what we sell, Frank.
Frank That's why ——
Alan That's why this is the shift where Bernard's started putting me in
charge.

Beat

Frank Today?

Beat

Alan Part of my ... general ... (*A beat; he swallows*) Yes.

Beat

Frank Right. Well.

They both get the score

Government didn't set up schemes for us to stand about chatting.
(*Heading towards the door*) Where d'you want me?
Alan WHOA whoa whoa, Frank. Just — whoa.
Frank Sorry. Jumping the gun.
Alan I'll need to give you the induction. Like Bernard gave me when
I / started ——

Frank Induction?
Alan Starts with the — (*he gestures to his nametag*) — everyone has
  to have a little ...
Frank Oh right. Nametag.
Alan Breaks down the invisible counter. Think there's one in my desk-k
  ... (*He rummages in an empty toaster box clearly full of stationery
  jumble. His head is practically lost in it*)

Frank clocks this is not really a "desk"

Frank It does *what* does it do, sorry?
Alan The invisible counter. The traditional ——
Frank Oh right.
Alan — kind of — (*he gestures at a "wall"*) — between staff and
  clients.
Frank I see. It's a metaphor.

Beat, where Alan thinks — "y-yeah, it might be ..."

Two "l"s in "Tollit".
Alan We tend to just put the first name really.

Frank goes to take it

No, no no. Company — "thing", this actually. Should feel like being
  awarded a medal.
Frank Oh right.

*Alan puts his hand out. Frank looks at it, and shakes it. Alan then tries
to pin the badge on*

Does anyone ever use them?
Alan Mm?
Frank Our names. I mean does anyone ever actually come in and say
  "I'd like to buy a kettle, *Maureen*"?
Alan We have a philosophy to put friendship over finance.
Frank (*nodding*) Alliteration.
Alan ⎫ (*together*) ⎧ (*wrestling with the tag*) Gn-urgh.
Frank ⎭   ⎩ They're very good, these, whoever writes 'em.
Alan Just need to prise it ...
Frank It's not really "friendship" you're wanting, though, is it? You
  don't want people hanging round the hoovers telling you about their
  allotment.

Alan (*struggling a little*) Gddssake..

Frank It's more a — "patina" of friendship. (*Beat*) A sheen.

Alan OW.

Frank Oh hey are we in trouble with that?

Alan (*"I'll get another"*) Mrrmmff ...

Frank Come on, it'll be all right. Give it here. (*He clicks, paternally*) Just nip and get me some ——

Suddenly it's the old tone he had with Alan on the ledge. Not the tone for an assistant to use to a boss

(*Almost inaudibly*) Sorry.

Odd moment. Alan gets out his walkie-talkie

Alan (*into the walkie-talkie*) Judith I'm going to be tied up doing a short induction.

There is no response. He pretends for Frank's sake that this is not the case

OK so what I have to do, Frank, is introduce you to the basic operating principle for all primary interface personnel. It's what ——

Frank (*frowning*) For what is it?

Alan For staff who are the first point of interface with clients as they walk in the ——

Frank "Salesmen"?

Alan Well no, 'cause we don't use the w ——

Frank By "client" d'you mean "customer"?

Alan No! See, 'cause — (*He points proudly and smiles*) "A customer gives custom. A client gives commitment."

Pause. Frank does an "oh, right" of the face

The whole thing is a total, total art. And I mean a lot of people, when they come in a shop, a lot of people look at store assistants and are just — "Oh God — (*shrugging*) — I could do that."

Frank (*nodding*) Absolutely. (*Pause*) Sorry, are you saying it's *not* —— ?

Alan It's not, Frank.

Frank No.

Alan I mean we went on a course.

Frank "You —— "?

Alan In a hotel. "The psychology of electrical retail".

Frank Wow. One of these weekend things, where everyone —— ?

Alan No, no, just over a lunchtime. They gave us all these psychological little clever little — see what you get is they take words we've got to remember, and turn the first letters into a word in everyday use. So the basic operating principle of Rocket is ... (*He writes "SPAPO" on the pad*) "SPAPO".

Beat

Frank "Spapo"?

Alan (*beat*) I mean it's not always a word in everyday use. Sometimes y' just can't.

Frank No. Well.

Alan So "S". "Smile". The face of "Rocket Electrical Superstores" is *always smiling*. They hate these droopy teenagers who moon about ...

Frank No well I can understand that.

Alan "P.A.". "Personal Attention". At the time you're talking to them, people should feel they're the only person in the world. And THAT's done with *eye contact*, OK? Keeping *eye contact*. And finally-y — "PO", "Personally Own".

Frank (*having a stab*) We share a sense of communal pride in the store?

Alan No. Whatever product someone's looking at, you say you personally own one.

Pause. Frank's concern makes Alan slightly ashamed of this last one

It's just one of the little — industry things that happens — (*swallowing*) I mean you DO want pride. *All* of this — (*he waves loosely at the list*) Bernard's like you about pride. He absolutely ——

Frank Me?

Alan Oh GOD. In fact when I came for me interview he threw me this curveball — said "what's the most important lesson y've learned in life, Alan"? And I kind of panicked and me brain went an' without thinking, I just said — (*mimicking Frank*) "Pride. Lesson one".

Frank looks at him. It's like an echo from a distant time

Apparently that's what swung it. All the other candidates said something about dishwashers. (*Beat*) So. Bearing that in mind, putting that into practice ... (*He gets a toaster from the hill of rejection*) ... let's just run a little role-play here. Say I came in to the store, OK, say I'm coming into the store and I'm the client an' I'm walking in and I say "I want a toaster". (*He puts the toaster on the chair*) What would you say?

Frank Right. OK. (*Beat*) How old are you?
Alan Doesn't matter.
Frank Male or female?
Alan Frank, toasters are unisex.
Frank No, I'm just building up a little character / of the ——
Alan I want a toaster. What d'you say?

Beat

Frank "Good. You should definitely have one".

Beat

Alan What else?
Frank A kettle.
Alan }
Frank } (*together*) No.
Alan Keep thinking "SPAPO".
Frank I'm thinking / that ——
Alan You're *smiling* ...
Frank (*smiling*) I am.
Alan (*pointing where nametag would be*) I can see that your name's Frank, so we've broken down that little ——
Frank (*nodding*) The invisible ——
Alan (*nodding*) The barrier. You've made the eye contact for the "attention" ...
Frank (*pointing at the toaster*) I personally own that.
Alan No you don't.
Frank One like it?
Alan No, what I'm saying — OK the "personally own" part, that's at the end.
Frank Right.
Alan That's a judgement you have to make during the sale interaction window ——
Frank (*"the what"?*) Whoa, sorry?
Alan — at the point where they're showing an interest. It's like a gear change in a car.
Frank Wow. It's quite a — (*he gestures at "fine line"*) ...
Alan Oh it is, Frank. The whole thing is a psychological ——
Frank — fine line.
Alan It's an art. I mean swap. Just swap roles ...
Frank So I'd be ——
Alan I'll show you. Say you want a toaster. You've come in the store and you say ——

Frank "Hello, Alan".

Alan Yes. Possibly. But "I want a toaster". Say ... (*Nodding, then slightly exasperated*) SAY "I WANT A —— "

Frank I WANT A TOASTER.

Alan (*"doing" it*) OK. Certainly, sir. Here's our range of toasters. They start with your very basic model and go up through your more stylish ones right up to this — (*with a wry smile, winking*) — "bread and patisserie management system". (*He points straightaway*) Now did you notice what I did there?

Frank When?

Alan Just run that back. What I did. Just see if you can pick out all the things I was subconsciously doing.

Pause

Frank N-no.

Alan (*relishing the chance to show off*) I gave three options, OK. I gave you "Basic". "Stylish". And "Over The Top". Each of these had a subliminal accompanying facial gesture. "Basic" was ... (*pulling a "slightly disapproving" face*) ... as in "no one wants to be thought of as 'basic'. 'Basic' people watch television with their mouths open". "Stylish" had a little ... (*doing a tiny wink*) ... as in "That's you. We both know that's what you are". And finally "over the top" had a slight ... (*With a wry smile, "tcha"*) ... little ... (*He does one again, "tcha"*) ... which is like — "honest, I WORK here and even I can't believe we sell these!" (*He gestures*) And *shazam*! In one speech I have raised you above the common herd, complimented your intelligence, proved I'm not trying to sell you the most expensive and in the event directed you towards the model on which we have the biggest mark-up!

Pause. There is a look from Frank which somewhere deep in his soul disquietens Alan a little

So I'll just nip and get another nametag off Judith. If you want, perhaps, while I'm gone, maybe want to er — generally ... (*He gets out a pen*) Reflect? On all that? Maybe take some notes?

Frank takes the pen. There is a slightly awkward pause

Frank Very smart.

Alan It was an award. "Employee of the quarter". (*Pause*) Y' get a pen.

There is a short pause

Personalized.

That didn't put much fairy dust on it

Alan goes

Frank looks at the pen

Alan comes straight back in

Also it's not just a pen. The other end's a screwdriver.

That didn't put much fairy dust on it either. Frank smiles a "great". The lack of fairy dust is apparent to both

Alan goes

Frank takes off the other end. He sits. He raises the pen up. He gets out his dictation machine from his lunchbox

Frank "Frank Tollit turned the screwdriver in his young, agile fingers. The mission, should he choose to accept it, was fraught with danger. "Build a fish tank using only Meccano and four windows from an abandoned Hillman Imp." (*He smiles to himself*) He hadn't shown the slightest interest in tropical fish 'til that ... Matterhorn of road grit got delivered to Cartwright's Aggregate Yard on the Dewsbury Road. (*His tone is effortlessly chatty, as though talking to his mates in the pub*).This, his friend Tony decided, was perfect for the bottom of a fish tank. Sadly that wasn't an opinion shared by the owner. As Tony and Frank were filling their anorak pockets the large, ex-fairground prizefighter Massey Cartwright emerged from the despatch hut. A shout volleyed across the Dewsbury road. The two boys turned and shot up the mound. Or rather *Frank* did. Tony had been wondering why HIS pockets seemed bottomless and half-way up the north face of Mount Gravel he found out. Being a child of hand-me-downs, his pockets had holes in, an' half a ton of grit had turned his anorak into a lead waistcoat. It was pulling him down so hard his hand-me-down shoes were starting to fill with gravel at the back. The massive fist of Massey Cartwright was just about to grasp his ankle when *suddenly* ... hand clasped hand, and the shaking arm of Frank Tollit hauled the trembling Tony Bell to safety." (*He smiles. He presses replay*)
Frank's Voice (*on machine*) "... Frank Tollit hauled the trembling Tony Bell to / safety."

Alan enters looking hassled

Alan Right. So I'm in the shop.

Frank reacts as if caught out

Frank Yes, right ...
Alan Have you done notes?
Frank Up here. (*He taps his head*) Memory's a muscle, Alan. You start taking notes, it's the mental equivalent of installing a Stannah Stairlift.

Alan isn't sure he knows what one of those is

Alan So as I say. We're back in the shop, I want a toaster. Off y' go.
Frank Hello, sir. We have a wide range of toasters starting very basic and going up to some over-the-top French rubbish, but personally I suggest the ones on which we have the biggest mark-up.
Alan No ——
Frank All of which I personally own at ——
Alan WHOA.
Frank NO.
Alan Frank ——
Frank (*putting his hand up in guilt*) DON'T — sorry. Sorry. Don't have to tell me.
Alan Wait there.
Frank Shouldn't've said the word "mark-up". Cardinal mistake. Spoke the subtext.

Alan goes to his "desk"

Alan Can't really have mistakes like that, Frank. That's how we end up with siblings.

Alan rummages for a pen in another empty toaster box under his table

Frank (*frowning*) Sorry?
Alan People who "showed interest but left". S - I - / B ...
Frank (*getting it*) "S - I - B" ...
Alan Went into Orbit.
Frank "Ordered retail, but / insufficient —— ?"
Alan No, *Orbit*. The other electrical shop. Opposite Boots.
Frank Oh right.

Alan searches his "desk" for ties. Beat. Frank looks out of the window as he puts on his nametag

> Thought it might be another one of your little ... (*Looking out*) Unbelievable out there in't it now? Cinema and everything. (*Beat*) Great view this place. Must have the best view of the Folly in the whole of Batley. (*Beat*) And of course perfect for your rooftop concerts.

Alan looks at him — what? Frank means the guitar

Frank How's it going? The band?
Alan (*after a beat*) Good. Really good. Lots of gigs.

Beat

Frank (*gently*) You OK?
Alan (*after a beat*) So anyway, Frank, you've passed. (*He puts his hand out to shake Frank's*)
Frank Mm?
Alan Grade one training.
Frank When?
Alan Just now. That was it. You're now a "Client Service Director". Qualifies you for one of these. (*He hands Frank a tie out of a box*)
Frank (*on glass*) Have I got a job?
Alan Well I'm not in a position — I mean ... (*Pause*) You've got a tie.
Frank I've got a tie. Not *definitely* got a job, but I *am* a "director".
Alan We don't believe in the term "assistant". "An assistant needs assistance, a director gives out —— " did I put that there?

He means Frank's lunchbox on the desk. He picks it up

Frank Sorry. That's my pitta bread. Evening meal. Thought I'd bring pitta bread. (*Taking it off Alan*) Amazing things, pittas, I've always thought. One of those all-or-nothing foods. Warm them up and they're like magic carpets. Serve them cold and it's like eating a flip flop.

Beat. Alan looks at Frank, for a moment lost in magic carpets and flip flops

Alan (*holding out his walkie-talkie*) You're going to be tailing Judith.
Frank "Judith". Right. (*He takes it*) I'll spot her by her nametag.
Alan Yeah. Also she's the one who sits on her arse all day bitching about why she doesn't need motivational talks.

Frank detects a little of what has gone on. He takes the toaster, along with his lunchbox

Frank I'll put this across the way, shall I? Continue the clear-out? (*He readies himself and tightens his tie*) This is it, then. Into the breach. (*Beat*) Only the second time in my life I've had a first day.

Frank goes

Alan looks after him. He has a spasm of drive. He pictures the absent Judith — with some venom

Alan *SO*. Hello, *Judith*. Welcome to this evening's motivational ... (*Struggling for "le mot juste"*) "Lesson". (*Something more powerful*) "Burst" (*No, that's not right*) "Lesson". Which STARTS ... Lesson one. "Pride". (*He writes "PRIDE" across the pad*) Tonight's "Ten At Ten ..." PRIDE — what IS ... that? What is pride made of? "P". "Purpose". Working here gives us a sense ... sense of purpose. "R". "Respect". For — (*no...*) "Reputation". Always remember the reputation of the Rocket name. (*He writes "REPUTATION" downwards. There isn't enough room. Under his breath*) Oh for God's sake. (*He stands back to reveal the letters of "reputation" get smaller to the point of illegibility*) "I".

Pause. He can't think of one for "I"

(*Start again, start again*) "D". "Deep". A real deep sense of ... er ... of ... (*He turns the easel to the window and draws a quick fluid line on the paper. We don't see it ...*) A deep sense ... (*... but it makes Alan smile. Possibly with a little pride*) "E". What I got in GCSE English.

Alan goes over to the case and pulls out a guitar. He starts to play the song he played a few years ago. Only at a more lyrical pace. And this time in a suit

> You made your bed now it needs lying in
> You put your chips all down on black ...
> You burnt the bridges on your Rubicon
> And now there's no going back.

It's a pool of calm. And memory. Somewhere a door to a garden has opened and Alan stares into it

Frank returns

Alan is still staring when

Frank Alan? Sorry. I just ——
Alan I said "tail Judith".
Frank Well that's the thing, see.
Alan ⎫ *(together)* ⎰ Just press the ——
Frank ⎭   ⎱ She sent me back.
Alan *(after a beat)* She did what?
Frank She said I should take a longer break because of having to stay
behind after work. So I didn't know where ——
Alan She said that?
Frank — where people go to eat if they brought their own.
Alan Seriously, she just said that, just then?

Beat

Frank I mean I don't think she was ...

Beat. Frank is aware he has been the unwitting bearer of bad news

Am I right to have me tea, then? (*Pointing out of the door*) Was I right
to warm me pittas?

Frank is worried about Alan. With an insect-like buzz, the letters **C** *and*
K *come on. He sees Alan's rucksack. He moves it to the base of the*
throne

Three steps to heaven. Never miss a meal. Never pass a toilet. And
always have your tea when the street-lights come on.

Frank sits and gets his meal out. Maybe food is a glimmer of light in
a dark world. Alan gets his lunchbox, and slowly starts to eat. Side by
side, same time as Frank

Y've packed that neatly.

Beat. Alan shrugs

Alan *(muttering)* 'S just logical. (*Pointing*) Don't want the yoghurt on
top of the cake 'cause it'd pressure down and mis-shape it.
Frank   *(nodding and pointing)* Also your lighter objects, your
Homewheat and your Jaffa, they need to go on the top, being fragile.
Which just about leaves space there for the apple / which ——
Alan *(nodding)* — which of course / is then ——

Frank — then protected from the water flask BY the cake ——
Alan 'S like a cushion really ——
Frank — minimizing the risk of / bruising.
Alan (*nodding*) Stops it bruising. (*He looks at Frank. With quiet horror*) Oh my God I've turned into you.
Frank (*nodding*) Two kinds of people in life, Alan. Those who get their lunchbox in order at breakfast, those who end up three hours later with bent cake and a V-shaped sandwich.
Alan What the hell —— ?

He pulls out the old dictation machine from Frank's lunchbox

(*Pressing a button*) It never still works, this? (*He briefly presses rewind, then plays it*)
Alan's Voice (*on the machine*) It never still works, this?
Frank There you go. Your grammatical inaccuracy preserved forever. (*Taking it back*) Borrow it for your band if y' like.
Alan Y've still not heard of the digital age?
Frank This IS digital. (*He presses the button*) You press it with your digits.
Alan The band split up.
Frank (*nodding, "oh I see"*) "Artistic differences", was it? You wanted to stay as was, the rest wanted to start playing recognizable tunes?
Alan Surprised you even remember what it sounded like.
Frank Oh you don't forget a noise like that, Alan. It's like people who've lived near abattoirs never forget the sound of dying bullocks.

Alan smiles

You could've formed another one. (*Beat*) Could've called it "Alan And The Neat Lunchboxes".
Alan (*with a wry smile*) Leave it out, Frank.
Frank (*ditto*) Hey. I'm proud of y'.
Alan (*after a beat*) Chloe didn't want a guitar cluttering the flat if I wasn't gonna be playing it.

Frank nods ruefully. He looks to the easel

Frank That an indelible pen? (*He gets his nametag out*) Judith pointed at me nametag and said "that's an unusual name for a man" and I said "is it?" and then realized the "k" had rubbed off ... what's this? (*He looks at the easel, in wonder*) Did *you* do this or did it come with the pad?

Alan just eats

(*Looking to the view*) You've got a real — (*gesturing*) — swoop to the landscape. The way y've got Preston's Folly up there like a lighthouse. That's all one line, isn't it?

Alan doesn't answer. Frank looks at the pen

Frank Should sign it. Important to have your name on things.

No response

(*Re: the nametag*) See if there's a pen for these across the way. (*He goes to the door*)
Alan Doesn't make me an artist, Frank. (*Beat*) I know y'd like to think.

Beat

Frank Did it make you happy?

Alan looks at him

Then it made you an artist.

Frank opens the door and is faced with a wall of thick smoke. He shuts it again as though that might have been a nightmare they both just saw. He goes to open the door again to double check

Alan (*shouting*) DON'T!

Frank freezes

CALM!
Frank I am.
Alan No, "CALM". We've got an acronym for panic management.
Frank Thought you might.
Alan Oh my God ohmygod — (*He grabs the remote control off Frank*) Walkie-talkie. "C". "Confirmation to manager". "A". "Alert staff".
Frank How do they do / that?
Alan (*punching the remote*) Secret code word. (*Into the remote control*) Judith this is Alan. Mr Alert — is in — the building. Repeat in the building we have a Mr Alert.
Frank (*sneaking a look through the door*) Not exactly the Enigma, is it?
Alan Judith? This is — DON'T, FRANK! (*Into the remote control*) JUDITH, THIS IS ALAN. ARE YOU RECEIVING ME? THIS IS ALAN. THIS IS ALAN. THIS isn't a walkie-talkie.

Frank immediately stiffens with guilt

Frank Now then. You see, what's happened there — (*pointing*) While I've gone to warm me pittas, I must've put the walkie-talkie down and picked up a television remote control.

Beat. Alan slides open the rear window

Alan "L" is leave.
Frank Which do look similar ——
Alan The building.
Frank In fairness.
Alan We need to leave the building. (*Calling*) JUDITH! (*He hangs over the edge, holding on to the* **K** *to steady himself*)
Alan } (*together*) { JUDITH!
Frank }   { Don't ——

The **K** *goes on the tilt*

Get off the letters!
Alan FRANK, I —— (*He backs into the* **C** *which wobbles dangerously*)
Alan } (*together*) { Bloody hell!
Frank }   { Seriously, I looked before and I don't ——
Alan FRANK THE ONLY LETTER THAT MATTERS NOW IS "M", WHICH IS "MAKE SECURE" AND I HAVE TO DO THAT BECAUSE I AM IN CONTROL O ——
Frank LOOK OUT!

The large **O**, *made to look like Saturn, starts to drop backwards. Frank leaps to support its decline back into the room*

Alan } (*together*) { Don't let it break. DON'T LET IT BREAK!
Frank }   { Steady! Support it, support it ...

They let it lower gently, gently, easing it down from the inside of the **O** *to a stop around their waists so it doesn't jolt on the hinge*

Frank ... not going anywhere. Support it. SUPPORT ... It's not going anywhere. (*Beat, he pats it*) There. Pristine.

There is a sudden explosion from the base. The letter lights up

Alan Thank God. It still works. God, if this had broken, I ——

Frank (*wide-eyed*) DON'T MOVE.

The urgency of tone makes Alan start

    (*Very measured, not moving*) Chances are they won't've fitted a P-nine.
Alan Which is?
Frank Isolator. Electrical isolator.
Alan So what —— ?
Frank It's live.

There is another explosion at one side. They both jump

Alan (*beat*) Which — bit / of —— ?
Frank Anything metal.

Another explosion at the base. They look down at the bright silver metal inner rim which they're practically touching on all sides

Alan (*swallowing*) How "live"?
Frank (*"staying still"*) Just look at me. (*Pause*) Can't be less than four
    hundred and seventy volts.

Pause

Alan Is that a lot? (*Beat*) I mean is it like Fahrenheit? What's four
    hundred / and —— ?
Frank At Forshaw's I once saw a bloke touch a ring spur at three
    hundred. When we found him, his teeth had been blown straight out
    of his gum.

Another explosion at the other side

Alan } (*together*) { (*going to shout*) JUDE ——
Frank }   { Don't ——
Frank (*with short, shallow breaths*) I'm almost touching. My hand
    down here's almost touching ...
Alan (*from a tighter chest*) Why wasn't there an ALARM? There's
    a drill every month. We know it's bloody WORKING. (*Pause*) She
    MUST know. This is the LAST — the absolute — this is the arse end
    of the building. Why was there no bloody alarm?

Pause

Frank You know that toaster?

Alan looks slowly up at him

Across the corridor? What might happen THERE — if you put
something in it. Like, say, anything. Bread. (*He swallows slightly*)
Pittas. It might've been sent back 'cause it wouldn't pop up? (*Beat*) You
might put something in it — it'd smoke and smoke 'til it overheated
and fused the plug. And then it would just ... stop.

Beat

Alan Is that what you did, Frank?

Frank is silent. Which is "yes"

Frank I think I can smell tuna.
Alan So. (*Beat*) Thanks to some burnt pitta bread I am now trapped,
out of earshot, at the arse end of a completely unused corridor in the
middle of an electrified letter "o". (*Beat*) The question has to be asked.
Could my first day in charge have gone any worse?

Pause

Frank In a minute I'm going to need a Jimmy Riddle.

Alan looks slowly at him

I always find when things are bad, imagine one step worse and ——
Alan Frank, / just ——
Frank (*with a change of tone*) Oh hello?
Alan What?
Frank Would you believe / it —— ?
Alan What're you doin'?
Frank By my hand. Down here! It *has* got a P-nine! They just didn't
bother to connect it. (*He is clearly performing minute movements with
his hands*) Too fiddly, you see. Devil's own job.
Alan Could you fix it now? Do it? You know to — how they work?
Frank (*on a point of honour*) I insisted putting P-nines on every letter
I ——
Alan No, but you *could*?
Frank Oh yes. With a screwdriver.
Alan (*after a beat*) OK well you stay here an' I'll just nip to B and Q.

Frank Weren't you employee of the month?
Alan You know what — can you not remind me of that right now?
Frank The pen. Didn't it have —— ?
Alan Screwdriver! It did! Does! Where did —— ?
Frank (*shouting*) DON'T —— ! (*After a beat*) Seriously, Alan, you can't
  move backwards. (*After a beat, nodding down*) Jacket pocket.

*Alan stops dead. He can't get it with his arms. Alan leans forward and
nudges Frank's jacket to one side with his nose*

Frank Can you see the pen?
Alan (*from inside Frank's jacket*) I can see — the pen.
Frank OK. Gently. Ver-ry gently ...

Alan bites the pen out of the inside pocket

  You got it?
Alan (*with his mouth full*) Mgg.
Frank OK, out it comes.

Carefully Alan brings the screwdriver pen out between his teeth

  OK. Now I've got my left hand by my left pocket. It's directly under
  the fall path of the screwdriver which'll weigh about fifty grammes, so
  it'll take about a second to fall a metre so if I start counting in regular
  seconds, and on "three" you open your mouth and on "four" I scissor
  my fingers, we should catch it. (*Beat*) Got that?
Alan Yep.

*The screwdriver drops out of Alan's mouth and clanks to the floor. Alan
and Frank look at the screwdriver on the floor*

Pause

Frank My fault. Shouldn't've asked a question.

Alan stares at it, mortified

Alan If you'll excuse me, I'm just going off to have a little time on my
  own. (*He slowly moves his head a centimetre to one side. Then slowly
  moves it back*) I'm back now.
Frank Will you tell me something, Alan? Do you think this will affect
  my chances of getting a job?

Alan looks at him

I just — I want you to know I wouldn't ask you to — skirt round this.
On my assessment. (*Beat*) You have to tell the truth. Which is that, in
life, some people aren't suited to some situations. And it may be ... that
I am not. For this. (*Beat*) But I tried, Alan. The most important thing
is that I tried. Because at my age if we stop trying ... we disappear. If
we stop trying we may as well zip up our belongings, settle our affairs,
say our farewells and draw our lives to a clo —

*Frank judders, appearing to have been electrocuted by touching the
letter*

Frank } (*together*) { ZZZZZZZZ-ZZ!
Alan }   { (*screaming*) NO-O!

*Which he keeps going quite a little while before dissolving into fits of
laughter*

Frank Zzzzt-t-arghahahahahaha! (*Beat*) One all. (*He lifts the letter
   back up, apparently now without any danger*)
Alan Not funny, actually. Not actually funny.
Frank No, it is, Alan. It really is.

*Frank heaves the **O** back*

It is now. And it was when YOU did it. (*Beat*) You weren't wrong
about that, either.

*The **O** is back in position, leaving the speechless Alan free*

In fact when you were sixteen, you weren't wrong about much. But
then none of us are, at sixteen. That's the sad thing, Alan. (*He turns*)
See, what you "don't know" at sixteen is fear. (*After a beat*) We get
older. We learn fear, we call it wisdom. By the time you're sixty you're
surrounded by so much bloody wisdom you can't move.
Alan (*re: the letter*) How did you do that?

Frank looks at the nametag in his hand

You did that — with a nametag?
Frank Rubbed some more off in the process, but hey. (*He turns his
   nametag*) This is "F" signing off. (*Beat*) Sorry. Probably a company
   ceremony for this, isn't there? "Return of nametag"? "Dismissal of

rejected apprentice"? (*Beat*) Probably called a DORA. (*He wipes the tag clean*) There you go. Ready for the next guy. Frank was never here. (*He holds it out. A beat*)

Alan I can't do this, Frank. (*He doesn't take the nametag*) Wasn't your fault.

Frank It's always your / f ——

Alan No. Bollocks. (*He points at the* **O**) That letter ... that's just — just contractors who don't know what they're doing.

Frank keeps offering the nametag

Frank The toaster wasn't ...

Alan Frank ——

Frank Alan ——

Alan — it's your first day. I'm not going to fill in a report that makes it sound like you're clumsy.

Frank Alan ——

Alan Because yes, in answer to your question, it WILL affect your chances of getting a job.

Frank Don't make me work here, Alan.

Pause

Unless you attend a work experience they stop your benefit. (*Beat*) It's a new scheme.

Alan looks at him. He is now totally lost

Alan What are you doing here, Frank?

Frank (*hurriedly*) Hey, it wasn't deliberate. What I did. Any of it. I didn't do any of this deliberately. It's just ... (*Beat*) Clumsiness comes easy when you don't care. (*Beat*) Like a lad who once knocked everything flying in here, but put a drawing pen in his hand and he just ... (*Beat, to the pad*) He became a musician. (*Beat*) I couldn't repeat a thing you've told me today about this shop, Alan. But I could tell you the exact way Massey Cartwright's hand looked forty-eight years ago when it was clawing up a gravel mound. (*He smiles, he has to clarify*) I'm writing about two kids escaping up a gravel mound for my column.

Beat. Frank smiles

I've got a column. (*He beams*) I'm a writer, Alan. That's my real job. (*He hands over the nametag*) D'you know *The Yorkshireman*?

Magazine? (*Mimicking the Alan of old*) "Mostly about moles and dry stone-walling". Last couple of years it's had this column. "A Childhood In Batley". (*He gestures humbly: "That's me". He smiles*)

Beat

Alan Do they make it? (*Beat*) The kids? Up the gravel?

Frank (*smiling*) Well. What happens — there were two, you see. One of them had already got up to the top but the other, he had shoes that weren't actually his, they were too big on his feet. So what happens...

Alan They fill up from the back.

Frank (*after a beat*) They ... Yes, they ——

Alan Higher he gets, the deeper he gets dragged in.

Frank (*after a beat*) How d'you know that?

Alan It's the guy in the Black Sea, isn't it? Forget his name. Running to his boat, getting chased up sand dunes, the one bit of his disguise he hadn't checked was his shoes. Which is the twist, 'cause his dad was a shoemaker and it's ironic that shoes are gonna be the thing that kills him. But then his mate from right since kids is on top of the sand dune and this hand goes down.

Frank (*after a beat*) What's that?

Alan In't it the final scene of *The Vatican Inheritance*?

Beat

Frank Yeah. Well. I can't write about the Black Sea like that guy. (*After a beat*) But I tell you what. Bet he can't write about Batley as good as me.

Beat

Thanks, Alan. (*He stands, collects his things*)

Alan watches him a while

Alan Is there a picture? (*He is staring out, deep in thought*) This column? (*Beat*) They sometimes have them, don't they? On the top of columns. (*Beat*) Might look good. Simple kind of — (*he gestures*) ... pen. Of something that hasn't changed since your childhood. Like the folly. But then all this as well, the White Rose, so it's like — "new and old, things that've changed, things that never will".

Frank watches as Alan, with some industry, gathers the pad, the guitar and heads for the door... considers, then goes to the window exit instead

Frank Won't they notice you've gone?

Alan I'll just be another letter that went out, Frank. (*Beat*) The missing silent "A" in "Rocket".

Frank I like that. "The missing silent A in —— " (*Frowning*) *What*, sorry?

Alan This store?

Frank Right. Is "Rocket"?

Alan Why?

Frank (*after a beat*) Out of interest, what's the one opposite Boots again?

Alan "Orbit Electrical".

Frank Right. (*Slight pause*) See, you know what I've gone and done there. I've told meself I had to turn up on the twenty-second, at two o' clock at some shop that had something to do with outer space. (*Beat*) Probably a manager in there now wondering why his trainee hasn't turned up.

Alan smiles

Alan Is that a problem?

Frank (*looking at his clipboard*) I have to be signed by a manager.

Alan takes out his pen. He signs it

Alan Sometimes important to have your name on things, Frank.

Frank takes it. He looks at him

Frank In life.

Music starts as Alan and Frank look at each other. They shed their name tags. Then their ties

Then go out through the windows and descend to an unknown freedom

CURTAIN

FURNITURE AND PROPERTY LIST

ACT I

On stage: IN OFFICE:

Desk. *On it*: laptop
Chair

ON LEDGE:

Ledge
Back wall
Side wall
Large sliding window with view to part of office
Hooped descent ladder over side wall
Dog-eared flag reading "Forshaws"

Off stage: Huge red capital **F**, safety equipment (**Frank** and **Alan**)
Cables and safety equipment (**Frank** and **Alan**)
Practical iPod, CD box containing fold-up poster of
   a lizard (**Alan**)
Practical dictation machine (**Frank**)
Large red lower case letter **a** (**Alan**)
Large red lower case letter **o**, tea, fruit drink, two-pack of
   digestives, enormous number of Twixes (**Alan**)
Large red lower case letters **r** and **n** which slot together
   to form an **S** (**Alan**)
Large red lower case letter **r** (**Frank**)
 (**Alan**)
Large red lower case letter **l** (**Alan**)
Large red lower case letter **e**, letter (**Frank**)

Personal: **Frank**: toolbelt containing small flat head screwdriver,
   coin (in pocket)
Alan: watch

ACT II

On stage: Large windows
Huge bright orange capital **O** (made to look like Saturn),
   C and **K** (beyond windows)

Small hill of boxed electrical goods with crosses on,
  including toaster
Cheap desk
Two office chairs
"Lizard" band poster (on wall)
Acoustic guitar in beaten-up case
Empty toaster boxes containing stationery, nametag and tie
Rucksack containing **Alan**'s lunchbox

Off stage: Lunchbox containing dictaphone, clipboard (**Frank**)
                Pad of paper, easel, marker pens, walkie-talkie,
                  pen/ screwdriver (**Alan**)
                Television remote control (**Frank**)

Personal: **Alan**: nametag

LIGHTING PLOT

Property fittings required: nil

ACT I

To open: Afternoon exterior lighting, gradually darkening

Cue 1	**Alan**: *"ARE YOU WATCHING, BATLEY?"* *Bring up UV effect on letters*	(Page 29)
Cue 2	**Alan** exits *Black-out*	(Page 29)

ACT II

To open: Late afternoon interior lighting

Cue 3	An insect-like buzz *Bring up UV effect on* **C** *and* **K**	(Page 44)
Cue 4	Sudden explosion at base of **O** *Bring up UV effect on* **O**	(Page 47)

EFFECTS PLOT

ACT I

ACT II

Cue 14	**Frank**: "It's live." *Another explosion at one side of the* **O**	(Page 48)
Cue 15	**Frank**: "Anything metal." *Another explosion at the base of the* **O**	(Page 48)
Cue 16	**Frank**: "... blown straight out of his gum." *Another explosion at the other side of the* **O**	(Page 48)
Cue 17	**Frank**: "In life." *Music starts*	(Page 54)